Ivan Lendl's Power Tennis

As Told to Eugene L. Scott

F A Fireside Book
Published by Simon and Schuster
New York

Eugene L. Scott is co-author of
Bjorn Borg, My Life and Game

Photography by Kathy Finnerty, Eugene L. Scott, Linda Pentz and Carol Newsom

Copyright © 1983 by Eugene Scott

All rights reserved
including the right of reproduction
in whole or in part in any form
A Fireside Book
Published by Simon and Schuster
A Division of Gulf & Western Corporation
Simon & Schuster Building
Rockefeller Center
1230 Avenue of the Americas
New York, New York 10020

FIRESIDE and colophon are registered trademarks of Simon & Schuster.

Designed by *JUDY ALLAN*

Manufactured in the United States of America

Printed and bound by Halliday Lithograph
10 9 8 7 6 5 4 3 2 1

Library of Congress Cataloging in Publication Data
Scott, Eugene L.
    Ivan Lendl's power tennis.

"A Fireside book."
1. Lendl, Ivan, 1960—   . 2. Tennis players—
Czechoslovakia—Biography. I. Title,
GV994.L36S36   1983   796.342′092′4 [B]   82-16962

ISBN: 0-671-45908-2

To my mother and father, who taught me that a simple round ball has a thousand sides, personalities, and directions.

Ivan Lendl

To my mother and father—my sternest and gentlest critics. What follows flows equally from each.

Eugene L. Scott

Contents

Ivan Lendl
The Record Book

1977   French Junior Championship
        Wimbledon Junior Championship
        Italian Junior Championship

1980   Star of Czechoslovakia
            Triumph in Davis Cup Final

1981   French Open Runner-up
        Defeated John McEnroe in Czech vs.
            U.S. Davis Cup quarter finals.
        Canadian Open Champion

1982   Volvo Masters Champion
        WCT Dallas Champion
        WCT Forest Hills Champion
        Ranks #3 in the world on ATP
            computer
        Ranks #1 in the world on WCT Nixdorf
            computer

VITAL STATISTICS

Date of Birth:	March 7, 1960
Place of Birth:	Ostrava, Czechoslovakia
Height:	6'2"
Weight:	175 lbs.
Hair:	Brown
Eyes:	Brown
Shoe Size:	10½
Racquet Size:	4¾ Adidas, made by Kneissel Strung with 16-gauge gut at 72 lbs. Weight—367 grams, or 13.1 ounces unstrung
Shorts:	34" Adidas
Shirt:	42" Adidas
Endorsements Also Include:	Linea Zeta grips and luggage, U.S. Gut, Ben-Gay, Penn balls, L'Alpina clothing (in Italy and Japan), Boca West, Nashua Copiers (in Europe only).

Introduction-Foreplay

*W*ho is *Ivan Lendl? And why* his *technique* book? Lendl, who is the third-ranking tennis player in the world, does not yet have the fame and record of McEnroe, Borg, or Connors. But his recent record is better than those of all three. Lendl has beaten the mighty McEnroe the last four times they have met—each time an important occasion: the 1981 French Open quarter finals, the 1981 Davis Cup, the 1982 Masters, and the 1982 WCT Dallas Finals. His victory streak along the way is unparalleled in tennis annals—89 wins out of 92 matches, including 1982 triumphs at the Masters, Dallas, and Forest Hills.

If Rod Laver is the father of modern pro tennis, then Jimmy Connors, Bjorn Borg, and John McEnroe are his disciples. Now there is another. Ivan Lendl. The Czech super pro has added new dimension to the word *power.* The world's best juniors are quick to emulate their champion models—witness the two-handed revolution stirred by Connors and Chris Evert Lloyd. Already youngsters foresake grace, depth, and touch to pound the ball in relentless explosions as their new idol, Lendl, does. Until Laver, the game's stars represented a bizarre alchemy of stroking ability. One might own a fabulous rolling forehand but defensive backhand, another a fierce serve but unspectacular footwork.

Pancho Gonzalez, for example, had possibly the

greatest serve ever, but admitted his backhand was not an offensive weapon. Don Budge was blessed with one of the most brutal backhands in history but certainly was not as agile as Bjorn Borg. Laver, the only player in history to win two Grand Slams, was arguably the first player to "have it all."

He had a wicked left-handed serve, could hit winners off both forehand and backhand from anywhere on court, his volley was a savage rapier, and he was incredibly quick and dextrous. How could anyone improve on Laver? It won't be easy, and it may take a generation or two. But the process has already started. In a sense, the new space of development is like the old days of separate stroke superiority, but on a higher level. In 1974, Connors won Wimbledon and the U.S. Open with a never-before-seen brute force from forehand and backhand. He rarely came to net, and his serve did not have the sting or accuracy of Gonzalez's. But he was fast afoot and, like Gonzalez, a ferocious competitor. What separated Connors from the rest of the field was the uncompromising attack of his groundstrokes, which strafed the tram lines like a firefight. No one ever hit the ball harder. Until Ivan Lendl.

Borg replaced Connors as the world's number one because he could hit the ball with pace for longer than Connors. Borg's percentage tennis from the baseline was unmatched. Until Ivan Lendl.

John McEnroe took over from Borg as the world's number one because his sense of offense on serve and volley was unequaled. While Lendl's volley is yet immature, his serve is spellbinding.

His groundstrokes are never defensive parries. If a foe is foolish enough to take the net, Lendl's precision creates passing angles never before contemplated. And the speed of his groundstrokes is such that even when they are reachable, the net man is often frozen in place by the specter of the approaching cannonball.

Lendl is not as supple as rivals Borg, McEnroe, or Connors; but he is taller and has longer arms, giving him a range that is deceptively comprehensive for so big a man. (Lendl is 6'2", 175 lbs.—the largest dimensions for any superstar in twenty years.) One side of a singles court measures only 27-by-60 feet, however, and only a third of that area is commonly used. Lendl dictates the flow of the match with a stroking cadence that borders on violence—which puts his opponent on defense. When a foe is forced to scramble in the backcourt from side to side, his returns are aimed for the center of the court just to stick in the rally. This reduces Lendl's required court coverage even further.

Lendl is the heir apparent to McEnroe's throne, and many experts think that even if the Czech superstar has not yet been crowned by the computer, he is already better than his American rival.

This is not to say Lendl's game is the ultimate. But it does represent a link to future advances in technique and style. One day soon, tennis will see a superstar with the defensive skills, consistency, and implacability of Borg, the volley and athleticism of McEnroe, the return of serve and fight of Connors, and the shot velocity and control of Lendl. Ivan Lendl represents the start of a new era in the endless search for the mythical perfect tennis player.

The only biographical notes in the pages that follow are those that relate to the methodology of his strokes and his resolute mental fiber (which may determine a player's essence more than his strokes). Whatever the shortcomings of the book may be in terms of being incomplete, remember that the protagonist has barely started his adult tennis-playing life—his talents are still blossoming. This book is his. And the beginning.

Tuning Up

"I don't like to lose in anything."

Ivan Lendl

I *have one prime criticism of current tennis in-*
struction books—the pictures are taken in static,
noncompetitive settings. For example, the pro is
asked by the photographer to hit a forehand, a
backhand, serve, etc., and the pro, conscious that
the world will soon be watching his form and
technique, primps as if he were in front of a mirror. He dresses up his shots as if they were going
to the prom—with long, exaggerated follow-
throughs, knees perfectly bent. This gives the
reader a false idea that the game is symmetrical.
Tennis is not symmetrical. It is a game of motion.
There is no such thing as a perfect bounce. This
is not golf, where the ball sits motionless waiting
to be struck. The player is moving, the opponent
is moving, and the ball is moving in three directions at once—determined by its own spin, its arc,
and its forward velocity. Because a ball never
bounces in exactly the same place at the same
height or the same speed, strokes cannot be
measured in posed perfection. Thus the photographs used here have all been shot in competitive situations. So if I look awkward sometimes,
I'm afraid that's a true portrayal of tennis.

There is a story that Hall-of-Famer Bill Talbert
tells about an Australian protege he took to an af-
ternoon instruction clinic. Talbert asked him to
describe the technique of his forehand. The Aus-
sie, whose forehand power was devastating, said,

Three examples of tennis's asymmetry. A speeding ball too close to my body forces a cramped forehand hit facing the net from the back foot and a backhand struck also from the back foot without moving into the ball—also I lose control from both feet being off the ground.

hesitatingly, "Well, I, ah, ah, take the racquet back and just, ah, have a go."

The young pro had no conscious understanding of the mechanics of his own stroke in terms of foot pivot, shoulder rotation, and so forth; Talbert's experience has been repeated often by teaching pros to disparage the teaching skills of the touring pro. Yet there is a current wave of thinking that holds that the apparently primitive expression "have a go" is not farfetched. First, the Zen concept of teaching, popularized by Tim Galwey's *Inner Tennis,* insists that the brain operates far faster than any conscious attempt to structure stroke patterns. For instance, if you miss a first serve, you don't go back to the baseline and ruminate carefully, "I must rotate my grip slightly counterclockwise to the backhand, throw the toss higher, and adjust my ready position." Instead, you simply take a deep breath, throw the ball up, and hit it. In other words, your brain has made the adjustments for you—if you hit the first one long, the message has already been programmed to hit shorter.

Second, imitation has arguably been determined by many experts to be more effective than words. For example, watching the pro hit a forehand is a clearer, quicker instructive device than listening to his explanation in stagnant detail. And third, although the benefit of teaching the proper fundamentals to a beginner has never been seriously questioned, trial and error is the only way a stroke will be perfected. Every student's learning curve soars (or drifts) at varying speeds and heights. Personal shortcuts are taken to abbreviate the painful learning experience. Everyone's shortcuts are different. That's why my backswing is executed with a closed racquet face and Sandy Mayer's with a wide-open face. Both of us hit with topspin, but we have arrived at different conclusions as to the most efficient method.

Personally, I do remember only three things that my first coach, Olvrich Lerch, told me. (1) To watch the ball. (2) To hit on the rise. (3) If you get a short ball or a clear shot at a winner, go for it. Hit the ball hard at this stage and you won't think about choking. In other words never push the ball when you can belt it. These were invaluable lessons, but scarcely constitute volumes of instructions. Pictures are the closest thing to watching me play—thus the emphasis here on photographs rather than words. Like the young pro, I feel that I just take the racquet back and "have a go."

The macro-adjustments to a service motion if I start to miss too many are common sense. If the ball is going into the bottom of the net, anyone's brain will automatically make him adjust his stroke to change the ball's trajectory. The specific engineering of that adjustment I couldn't possibly tell you—and I doubt if anyone else could either without a computer printout of a stress/power/stroke graph of each mistake. The variables are endless, and possible corrections for each mistake add another multiple of answers. And since top teachers vary by 180 degrees on many important stroking principles, my advice is to take a shortcut. Calculate what works for you by experimentation.

Famous former Australian Davis Cup Captain Harry Hopman has recently guided the training of

Vitas Gerulaitis, Paul McNamee, Fritz Buehning, Yannick Noah, and Peter Fleming. He disagrees with prominent teacher Vic Braden who insists that a player cannot really watch the ball. Now watching the ball is a basic bit of advice that every student of every game is taught immediately. Braden now has photographs that attempt to prove his interpretation, which is that even a top pro can't come close to seeing the ball make contact with the racquet. Hopman disagrees. Where do I stand? I don't think the argument is worth it. The issue is concentration, not being able to see the seams on the ball. What works for you? Try staring at the ball with a lazer's gaze for five minutes or so. After a while you realize that rigid stare would wear you out or make you a nervous wreck—or both—even if you were able to sustain the effort.

Concentration is critical to the extent that you never become preoccupied or distracted by things happening around you. When I say "never take your eyes off the ball," I'm not saying it's important to read its label; but it is crucial to follow the ball's flight from the opponent's hand to his service toss. It's not good enough to begin to watch the ball in mid-flight.

There are only six pictures on pages 101–3 in this text that have not been taken during match play. They were taken for comparison purposes. Can you see the difference between the relaxed model posing for a volley and the strain of competitive reality?

Czech Point

"Ivan Lendl is the only East European who ever believed he could be the No. 1 player in the world."

Wojtek Fibak

I have been accused of not being communicative with fans or the press. It's true. I think more than I talk. The press does ask some silly questions.

I *started playing tennis uncommonly early. Be-*ing an only child helped. My father, Jiri Lendl, is a lawyer in the coal mining city of Ostrova which has so many smokestacks it is called, not so affectionately, "the black city of Europe." Father was once ranked among the top fifteen Czech tennis players, and I struggled almost obsessively to beat him, which I did finally when I was thirteen.

But my mother, Olga, was even a more pressing force in my tennis fortunes. Olga Lendlova attained the number two ranking in Czechoslovakia. She went to her tennis club every day to practice and brought me along. I was only three. But I started to hit even then with a wooden paddle. Neither parent pushed me. They let me play as much and as often as I enjoyed it. They never forced me to practice. If I told my mother I wasn't going to play tennis one day—that I was going to the zoo—her only question was, "Who are you going with?"

Their attitude was correct. If I had any advice to parents bringing up potential tennis players, it

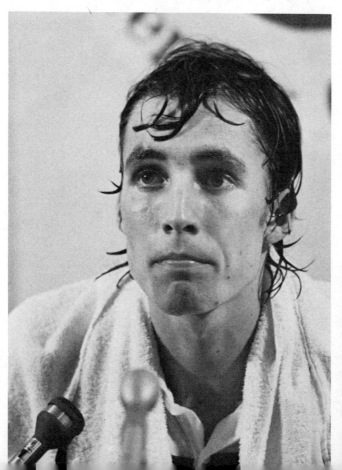

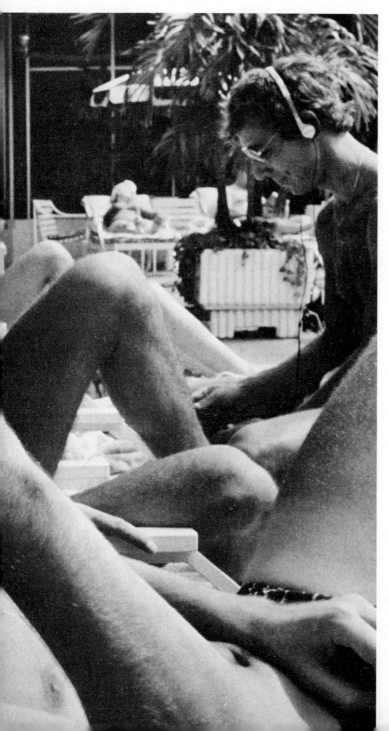

But I can relax . . .

and relax.

would be, just make the game accessible. And then stay away and let the coaches do the work. Don't hover over your children and don't press them.

My parents' philosophy carries over to my practice habits today. I think they were right. I only practice when I want to. If you do otherwise, you're just kidding yourself. The session won't help at all if you're not keen. The best days for learning are those when you really want to play. You try new shots, you feel confident, and you play well—and these factors reinforce themselves.

On the other hand, no one feels like working every day. And face it, the tennis court is my office. If a youngster wants to rest a few days every two weeks, fine, but if the ratio is reversed and he wants to take off fourteen out of fifteen days, he doesn't have any interest. Forget him. For tennis anyway.

I think it's important for kids to have a variety of sports to pick from when they are young. So if they finally select tennis it should be by choice—not lack of choice. I enjoyed other sports when I was young, including soccer, ice hockey, basketball, swimming, and skiing. Also I used to roller-skate to the tennis courts every day.

Since everyone is looking at the bad behavior of some superstars and teenagers and questioning where it begins and how it can be corrected, let me make this comment. I used to mope around the court when I was young. I was angry that I had put so much hard work into the game and was still losing. I never screamed or fired my racquet (because I only had one) but I would get furious at myself. Several times my mother sent

me off the court when I misbehaved, and her dis-
cipline helped in the long run. First it embarrassed me to have to leave the court, and second I
soon realized that getting upset hurt my concentration. I didn't behave better because I wanted to
get a gold star. I shut up because all my own noise
and turmoil affected my game. It was strictly a
practical solution. Besides the tantrums made me
look like a jerk.

When I was fourteen I beat my mother for the
first time. This was certainly the result of my being
part of (starting at eight years old) what is known
in America as the "Czech tennis factory," which
has produced a disproportionately high number
of champions—Jan Kodes, Martina Navratilova,
Hana Mandlikova, and Tomas Smid—considering the size of our country.

In the United States the junior tournaments—
except the nationals—are fragmented into seventeen sections. In Czechoslovakia, all the top juniors play all the tournaments in the summer, so
the competition is intense—eight weeks consecu-
tively, two tournaments a week, singles and doubles. This amounted to hundreds of matches,
which helped build my mental strength. What
consolidated that strength was traveling around
the world at fifteen and sixteen not knowing anyone, often not understanding the language—although I now speak six, Czech, English, Polish,
Russian, German, and Slovak—and not having
anyone help me. Self-reliance becomes as in-
grained on the tour as eating and sleeping.

*Ivan Lendl is totally free to travel when and where
he wants, primarily because of the easing of his*

country's visa restrictions following the defection of Martina Navratilova in 1975. In 1982, Lendl will earn close to two million dollars on court alone. He will return to the Czech Tennis Federation approximately $300,000 as part tax, part license for permission to play the world circuit. Though he does own a condominium at Boca West, Florida, with several other touring pros, including Marty Riessen and Tim Gullikson, Lendl considers Prague, where he has bought his parents a house, his home.

I know as I have become more successful, I have been criticized by the press for being, at various times, curt, sarcastic, reclusive, cold, impolite, and condescending. Part of the problem, I admit, is not enough tolerance on my part of the press who ask me such foolish questions as, "What was the turning point of the match?" (Don't they know?) or "Were you disappointed after losing?" (No, I was rather pleased?) or "What are your goals?" The press want me to behave like an American and don't understand if my values are different. Europeans are not aggressive in their conversation. They do not talk about their money or success—or about being number one. When a journalist asked me at Dallas after beating McEnroe whether I thought I was the best in the world, I said, "My answer is in two parts—'no' and 'comment.' You put the words together."

I have always said that winning the next match was the most important thing. Of course, I want to win Wimbledon, the French Open, and the U.S. Open. But if you set a goal and you make it a do-or-die situation, you don't leave much if you lose.

There's a lot of losing in our game. Imagine if Wimbledon or the French had been the only important goals in life for every tennis player in the world during the five- and six-year respective reign of Borg. If so, 600 pros would have considered themselves failures, including myself, which I think is ridiculous.

There are so many things that can stop you from winning: an injury, a match point and a let cord loser, bad luck, or simply a bad match. If I say I must win the French Open and don't, it could affect my performance at Wimbledon. Personally, I don't think it's the end of my career if I don't win a particular U.S. Open. If I have a bad loss I try to forget about it. I also try not to have one goal—other than the general one, which is to win every match. I feel players may fall into the trap of having their ambitions articulated by the press.

There is one aspiration that is a constant—playing Davis Cup. It is important to me and important to my country. A brief political turmoil this year pointed up how Davis Cup is different. I got myself into a terrible conflict of trying to honor two commitments during the same week at Forest Hills and the Nations Cup in Düsseldorf. My government was totally understanding of the mixup and supported my conclusion not to play the Nations Cup by saying it was totally my decision. Davis Cup would have been another story.

My rivalry with John McEnroe? I hope that I don't let the hostile tone put by the press on the rivalry get to me. I want to go out and beat whoever is on the other side of the court, whether it be my best friend Wojtek Fibak or McEnroe. It doesn't matter who. The press has made a big deal out of my hitting McEnroe and knocking him down with the ball in Dallas this year. I also did the same thing to Vitas Gerulaitis at a crucial stage of the 1982 Masters. I won the point both times.

My judgment is that there are only limited options when a rival is at net. I can pass down the line, hit crosscourt, lob, or hit straight at him. A few years ago, I concluded I was losing too many sure points at close range by the netman outguessing me down the line or crosscourt. I needed an alternative and discovered it by accident in mis-hitting a hard crosscourt drive that went straight down the middle. My opponent missed the shot, even though it was within reach, because the route of the ball took it right under his right arm—which is the "jamming" side of the body. Then I started hitting the same shot on purpose. I aim for the right side of the stomach and hard. Contrary to what the cynics say, I'm not aiming for the head. It sometimes looks that way because any ball hit hard under the forehand arm causes an extremely awkward reflex. Try it and you'll see that your foe may fall down trying to get out of the way.

I also think a man comes to net at his own risk—certainly not at my invitation. And if he reaches the net, he should be prepared to defend it. It has always amused me in doubles to see that when a player is hit by accident, a bitter response is often provoked with each side trying to pound the other on every short ball. Revenge is a natural sentiment to feel toward a player who can't control his smashes well enough to avoid hitting an adversary. He must expect the consequences. I expect that if one of my forehands whizzes out of control and bowls my foe over that he's going to come swinging for me. The difference is that I won't get in his range if I've hit a short ball.

Donald Dell, my agent, has said that I have a drive to be number one for my family, myself, and my country. There is some truth in what he says, although I don't have an *obsession* with being number one. My opinion is that if you are determined and work hard anything is possible—or, put another way, nothing is impossible. But the faraway goal is not the real objective—the methodical day-to-day struggle is.

I would certainly include Wojtek in Donald's definition of family. Wojtek is my closest friend on the tour. Fibak is not, as many think, my coach. If he were my coach, he would have to be with me at all times preparing for my practice and matches. He was not with me at this season's Forest Hills final and for much of my preparation for the French. He has a life of his own and it's not as my coach. When we are together, we rarely talk about tennis. I have thought a lot about the concept of the coach and am determined I don't need or want one. After all, I'm out on the court alone. Why can't I win or lose by myself?

Forehead and Forehand

"Lendl hits the forehand harder than anyone I've ever seen . . . he deforms the ball when he hits it."

Arthur Ashe, Jr., U.S. Davis Cup Captain

*M*y forehand is not for everyone. My game is not for everyone. But if I give you two basic options—my way and an accepted alternative—you'll have a clear choice and may ultimately wind up somewhere in between. And personal choice is critical in tennis. Just watch any of the world's top ten hit a forehand—or anything else for that matter. No two hit the same.

The variations among the forehands of Jimmy Connors, Bjorn Borg, Guillermo Vilas, and Mats Wilander do not just boil down to insignificant details. Not only is the stroke preparation of each entirely different, but the result and purpose vary as well. Connors uses only slight topspin and aims for deep in the backcourt with extraordinary power and little margin for error, shooting for an outright winner or a helpless return. Borg employs excessive topspin with punishing pace, aims for midway between baseline and service line with excellent margin for error, and hopes to wear out foes with consistency or frustrate them into coming to net on a poor approach.

Vilas also hits with abundant topspin but less velocity and more arc on the ball than Borg. His plan is simple: to run his rival into the ground. Wilander, perhaps, is more flexible than the other three. He can hit with extraordinary velocity and has a better sense of the percentages than Connors when using his forehand to prepare his way to net. Connors' underspin approach, which rarely clears the net by more than an inch or so and often finds the top of the tape, has long been his undoing. Wilander, however, understands that the net is higher as you close in (obviously not higher in absolute terms but in relation to the greater angle required to get the ball over) and he adjusts his topspin accordingly. The Swede actually opens up the court with the shot while Connors is really just trying to lay the ball deep into the corner.

My forehand is entirely different from all four. It has been described as semi-western. Could this be something between Kenny Rogers and Buck Rogers? Labels can be distracting. In the same month this spring *World Tennis* and *Tennis Magazine* defined my forehand as semi-western and western. I don't use as much topspin as Borg, yet I hit harder than anyone—not deeper than Connors but harder. My purpose is more offensive

The grip in repose has little to do with the grip in action, yet photos do show basic finger positioning, particularly the extended index finger and thumb curling around and touching the middle fingers.

than Borg's, Wilander's, or Vilas', but not as risky as Connors'. I try to maintain a sound percentage and wait for the short ball when I am not afraid to fire for the winner. In effect, I regard a short ball the way a net rusher does a volley—as a chance to end the point. So you can see that variety is not just a matter of how you hit a ball, but where and why, too!

For example, the conventional wisdom on the forehand backswing is to take the racquet straight back. Yet biomechanic theory says that it is simpler to take the racquet back the way Sandy Mayer does, with an open face. On the other hand, I bring my racquet back with a closed face. See? Three different theories for the common denominator of all groundstrokes—the backswing.

Most top players—defying basic instruction adage—hit the forehand with an open or near open (body facing the net) stance and do not transfer weight in the classic fashion from rear foot to the

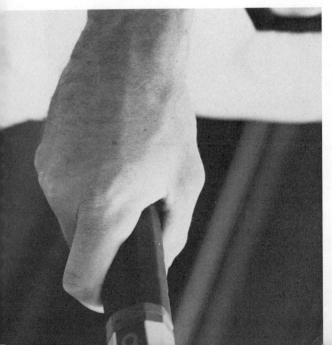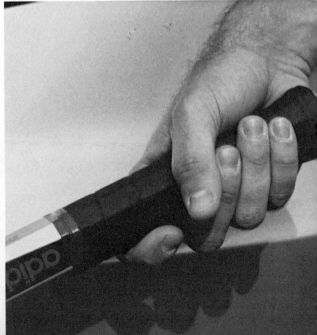

front foot. More than any other top-tenners, I do tend to fit the classic mold—not necessarily because I think it is more effective, but because that's the way I was taught and it worked for me. I always had a good forehand. I practiced very hard to get under the ball with the racquet, which because of its closed face was never easy.

Simultaneously with my right shoulder turn, I begin and complete the backswing with my racquet face parallel to the ground. The closed racquet face raises my elbow and forces the semicircle of my backswing to be greater than the slight arc of a straight backswing where the elbow stays very close to the side. The result of this exaggerated swing is increased racquet velocity, which adds to power on contact with the ball.

Obviously, as I begin my swing forward, the racquet face opens and I drop the head below the ball. More than any other top player, my racquet head is far below the level of my wrist. In fact, my

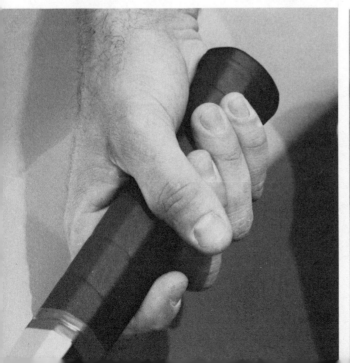
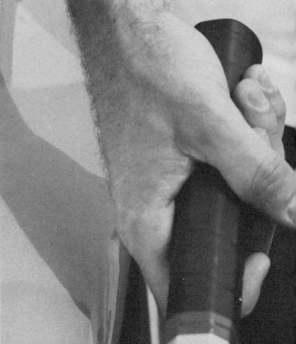

I take a long exaggerated backswing with a loop and closed racquet face almost parallel to the court—not conventional but effective.

racquet is frequently pointed at a rakish angle down toward the court as it comes forward to meet the ball. The flight path of my racquet is certainly not the conventional straight back/straight forward. There is a certain amount of wrist slap at the millisecond of contact, and my follow-through is exaggerated. The swing is upward, finishing a foot higher than my head. Note that my hips only move as a product of my entire upper body movement. In a sense, the hips only follow the action of my arms, legs, and upper body. Unlike

Five photos selected for their dissimilarity in body and foot position for balls approximately the same distance from contact. Different speed, spin, and height of approaching balls demand different techniques and often last-minute ad-

golf, the hips do not play a major part in producing power—the idea being that if every part of your body explodes forward like the swing in baseball or golf, power may be gained but control is forever lost.

My grip, which naturally begins the forehand relationship, is semi-western—that is, halfway between the exaggerated western forehand with the wrist directly behind the grip in the fashion of Borg, whose palm is partially under the racquet handle, and the traditional eastern grip used by al-

justments. But note important constants—elbow slightly bent and close to the side, cocked wrist behind grip, and racquet face flat and under the ball immediately before contact. Plus similar finger positions of idle left hand.

most all the top women, including Chris Evert Lloyd, Martina Navratilova, Tracy Austin, Andrea Jaeger, and Hana Mandlikova, with the *V* formed by the thumb and index finger directly over the top of the grip.

The rest of the grip is conventional—thumb somewhat pointed outward and three aft fingers close together, with a moderate separation of the index finger for feel. The most unusual element of my grip is not the finger arrangement but the fact that my hand chokes up on the handle, leaving the butt end slightly exposed. This enables me to

I am able to cross left foot over right in two out of three of these photos, and the ball is hit slightly in front of the lead foot—but see how differently I bend my knees depending on the bounce of the ball.

flex the racquet somewhat faster and to adjust more quickly to bad bounces. Don't believe the innuendos from other sports that if you "choke up" you're frail or a sissy. Experiment to find out what you're comfortable with. The minuscule loss of racquet length by choking up is unimportant compared to gaining proper balance and hand maneuverability.

Also don't be embarrassed by personal superstitions. I always hold my racquet with the Adidas label down (although for purposes of shooting

The slightly blurred racquet with the ball in perfect focus indicates the incredible racquet head velocity required to impart topspin. Also note that my eyes focus in front of the ball, indicating that I am probably not watching the ball at the precise moment of contact.

two of the grip photos I relaxed my stubbornness). There may be some sense in this quirk too. No racquet is absolute in its balance. But you can get used to the particular balance of each. In an effort to ensure as much continuity as possible, I always want to hit my forehand on the same side of the strings—same for the backhand, the serve, and all the strokes. Also I bounce the ball four times before my first serve and three times before the second. No reason. Just habit.

I am critically aware that the major weakness of my groundstrokes is footwork. At 6 feet 2 inches

Textbook balance—knees bent, moving forward into the ball—yet untypical. It is a rare photograph that does not show my racquet face below the ball, indicating a half volley forehand inside the baseline with a flat blocking action rather than topspin.

and 175 pounds, I am one of the tour's biggest men. Unlike Connors, Borg, Gerulaitis, and Wilander, quickness on the court is not one of my strengths—though I am constantly working on it by doing short windsprints both on and off court. Jogging is excellent for building stamina but the jogger's strides are unrelated to tennis, which demands short bursts of speed. As a result I try to prepare my strokes more quickly and precisely. Thus I turn my shoulder and begin my racquet backswing early. I am conscious of my body balance throughout the stroke. If I miscalculate the

Though the open mouth does not help the stroke, it's definitely part of my game.

Conclusive proof that my eyes are far ahead of the ball at contact.

pace, direction, or crazy bounce of a shot or am lazy in preparation, the awkward consequences are far more drastic than for smaller men.

Although coach Lerch did tell me to cross my left foot way in front of my trailing or right foot when I had ample time, there was no other advice. He just told me to hit it without specifics. At the beginning of my career everyone told me to hit flat. I developed topspin entirely on my own.

Excessive topspin in tennis has been authenticated in large measure by the success of Borg,

The moment of contact to the follow-through is just as important as the preparation (which has as many variations as there are players). Generally I do not bend as low on the forehand as on the backhand. Even if I do cross my left foot over my right properly, my body does face full front at the shot's completion.

who was able to win five successive Wimbledons
and six French Opens. Because his feats were ac-
complished on such contrasting surfaces—grass
and clay—violent topspin quickly became tactically mandatory for two basic reasons. First, it improved the margin for error enormously—the ball
cleared the net by yards and didn't tempt fate by
landing close to the base- or sidelines. Rallies
could be extended because of improved percentages, and sharper angles could be explored on
groundstrokes and passing shots. Second, that
dipping topspin was the perfect defense against
the aggressive net rusher. With the ball clearing
the net by a comfortable measure and dipping at
the net man's feet, the volley had to be hit up and
therefore defensively.

There is a third reason for the effectiveness of
topspin equal to the first two. Nothing is more
misleading than watching Jimmy Connors pound
groundstrokes from the baseline. Both his forehand and backhand are hit with very little topspin,
and his shots clear the net by precarious margins.
Average players watching Jimmy on television assume that if this technique is successful for
Jimbo, it is something they should aspire to.
Wrong. Jimmy Connors is an incredibly gifted
athlete. The penetration and precision of his
drives are unique. No one else on the pro circuit
can match Connors' low percentage yet spectacular accuracy from the baseline. You can't either.

Some of us on the tour equal and often surpass
Connors' spectacular aggression by another
means—torrid topspin which adds consistency
and fortifies one's confidence to stick in on each
point longer waiting for a surer kill.

The topspin's flight path accentuates a lesson in tennis that is often forgotten—that the ball does not travel in a straight line to get over the net. The ball goes up and drops down into the court in an inverted *V.* Hitting the ball with considerable top-spin reinforces the image of that "up and over" pattern more than flat groundstrokes.

One familiar trick question of the instructor is to ask his students to close their eyes and tell how much of the opponent's court they normally can see over the net. The answer, of course, is not 70 percent, not 50 percent, but nothing. That's right. At 6 feet 2 inches, when I am ready to serve, I can only see my rival's court *through* the net, not over it, which further reiterates the importance of think-ing that the ball must be lifted up and over the net. Topspin aids this thought process.

Backfiring the Backhand

"When I was eighteen, I won the French, Wimbledon, and Italian Junior Championships. I had no backhand at all."

Ivan Lendl

A *current wave of thinking insists that topspin* off both forehand and backhand is easier to learn and teach than underspin. The basis for such a hypothesis is that since the trajectory of every groundstroke is more like a mortar than a rifle (i.e., that balls must lift over the net and drop into the other court and do not go straight ahead like bullets), topspin performs this "lifting" and "dropping" function easier than underspin.

The theory works for the forehand because its movement is a very stable, if not forceful one. Test it yourself. Have someone resist the forward motion of your closed fist (by pushing against it) as it moves across your body, and repeat the exercise with your backhand traveling in the opposite direction—which is a far weaker action. The point is that the underspin backhand is possibly the easiest shot in tennis to master and one which most of the top pros revert to when in trouble.

When I say I had no backhand at all as a junior, it's not entirely true. I had a harmless chip backhand. I would rarely miss, but it could be attacked with impunity. I knew that if I were to succeed on the men's tour I needed to develop a riposte to the net rusher. Before I added topspin to my backhand, its execution was marvelously simple. The backswing was straight back with racquet head slightly elevated. The racquet would come forward from a low to high line in almost the identical trajectory the ball would follow. Though the

Excellent preparation (facing page). Racquet back early, good shoulder rotation and right foot in front of left, knees bent and proper balance for weight distribution to front foot.

My forefinger moves flush against the middle finger, thumb straight down, unlike the great Don Budge, whose thumb was outstretched horizontally along the side of the racquet grip.

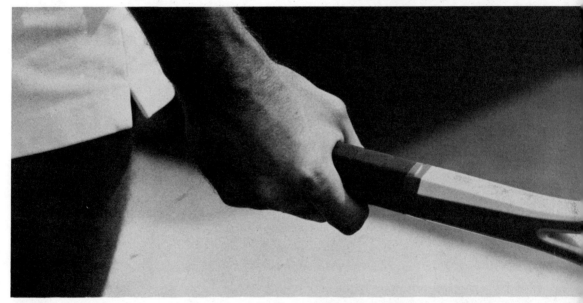

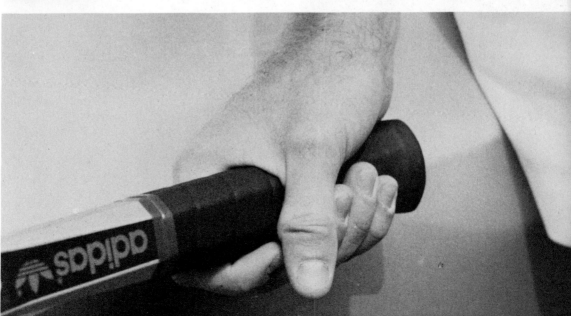

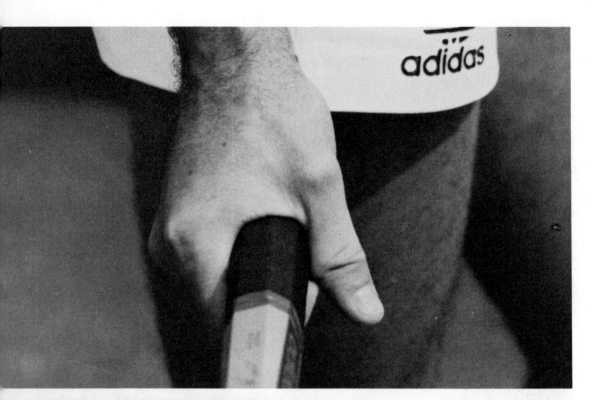

underspin backhand is in bad repute on the circuit as being too defensive and ineffective, it's an unfair rap.

Ninety-nine percent of all tennis is played on weekends for recreation, when steadiness is the principal if not sole weapon. Nothing is steadier than slicing backhands crosscourt. At the pro level, underspin, which lands short, invites attack. Its rising diagonal is a perfect target for the volleyer. But even at tournament level the underspin backhand is underrated. For example, from the same backswing, the lob, the dropshot, and drive can be executed. Disguise and consistency are the underspin backhand's prime attributes.

Three important observations: The butt end of the racquet extends past my palm (in contrast to many players whose hand entirely engulfs the grip); my fist points down toward the court in the backswing; and I use my left hand to help guide my racquet back.

But among world class players, only Ken Rosewall has succeeded in the past twenty years with just an underspin backhand in his repertoire. I did not anticipate being able to match Rosewall's laserlike precision. Thus for three years, starting at age seventeen, I worked on topspinning my backhand. Three things helped—hard work, choking up slightly on the racquet handle for greater flexibility, and the model of my friend Wojtek Fibak's rolling backhand. I am able to generate substantial power by a pronounced left shoulder turn, early and diligent preparation, and a fortunate combination of precision and timing.

I almost always hit the topspin backhand exaggerating the classic movements of the right foot far out in front of the left foot and proper weight transfer from rear to front foot. The most identifiable feature of my backhand is how low I get to

Preparation for my backhand is more intense than for my forehand. Though the backhand swing itself is more natural—in that it is not obstructed by the body—it is not as strong a movement as the forehand, which often can be flicked at the last moment. My knees are bent extremely low and my arm is straight.

the ball. My left knee is sometimes bent so low that it scrapes the court surface. Bending and staying low give my swing a stability it would not otherwise have. Occasionally I do smack the backhand with all my might, and instead of the stroke spinning me off balance, being close to the ground acts as a fulcrum and control point.

The arm pendulum starts the racquet below the level of the ball. The lifting topspin action is a combination of the upward and forward racquet motion and a slight body lift. My backhand back-swing is somewhat like the forehand except that the closed racquet face is not so pronounced and

I do use my left hand to help take the racquet back. I don't believe that the personal nature of my backswing is very relevant to my stroke or anyone's stroke unless you have a problem to correct. For example, if you need more power or if you're having trouble maintaining any rhythm, an exaggerated loop in the backswing may help. If there were a single most efficient way to take your racquet back, everyone would look alike on the court. For instance, even though my elbow flies high and wide on my forehand backswing, at the

Concentration is a must. Left hand simply hangs out of the way.

moment of contact, my elbow is very close to my side—almost identical to the more conventional eastern forehand.

Contact point is critical. So is the follow-through. As much as it is possible, considering the different joint and muscle arrangements, backhand and forehand motions from contact to follow-through are near mirror images—including dropped racquet face below the ball to a high fluid follow-through above the head. Contact point is obviously somewhat different, consider-

Follow-through is a product of ultimate ball direction, and so different body positions are inevitable. I tend to stay as low as possible to ensure my balance and control. This is not always possible, but one thing always is—a high racquet head follow-through.

                                         Ivan Lendl's Power Tennis

ing that the shoulder lines up the forehand with optimum contact point behind the backhand. It is therefore possible to hit a backhand farther in front than the forehand, although if you attempt to meet the ball very far ahead of the lead foot, in either stroke, strength and leverage are lost.

When I mention hard work, it is not idle talk. My version of western forehand demands intensive preparation, swing, and follow-through. The effort may be so intense that a player may be out of position or off balance afterwards. Consequently,

This is my follow-through for a high ball (photo taken on a hard court).

few players with western forehands had powerful backhands. Hall-of-Famers Billy Johnston, Maurice McLoughlin, Vic Seixas, George Lott, and Gardinar Mulloy all had relatively frail underspin backhands which were simpler to execute after a big forehand effort. The modern game will no longer tolerate such weakness.

One of my favorite examples of contradictory theories is the debate about whether to hit the ball on the rise, at the top of the bounce, or on the way down. My conclusion is that there is no absolute answer, although each player's ultimate choice characterizes his game. John McEnroe is the most talented of the modern players at hitting the ball on the rise; and he is the game's most aggressive star, taking great offensive risks. He both pays the price and reaps the rewards for his style. Jack Kramer and Jimmy Connors are ardent disciples of hitting the ball at the top of the bounce, and both consider relentless offense the key to success on all surfaces—although neither would gamble so boldly as McEnroe. Bjorn Borg inevitably hits the ball on the way down, and his selection is reflected in his near perfect application of consistency, power, and counterpunching.

My personal preference is somewhere between the second and third approaches. When I get an ideal shot to hit in terms of speed and height, I strike at the top of the ball's bounce. But if I am hurried or off balance or still trying to find my groove, I wait and hit the ball on the way down. Whatever *you* decide, it should fit the tapestry of your game. For example, it would be absurd to hit on the rise if you plan to spend all your time behind the baseline, or to hit an approach shot just before the ball bounces again. The sooner you hit the ball the more offensive your game, with its attendant pros and cons. The choice is yours.

At Your Service

*T*he beginning of the serve is naturally the grip. I use the same grip on serve as on my backhand, which is accepted instructional technique and one of the few "universals" in teaching that seems proper for everyone. Although a western or eastern forehand grip can generate both power and spin on forehands, it does neither efficiently on serve.

My set position on serve is to place the right foot directly behind the front foot. The trend started by John McEnroe, and imitated to some extent by other big servers Peter Fleming, Chip Hooper, and Yannick Noah, is to bring the trailing foot back to 7 or 8 o'clock (if you draw a single perfect circle around the foot placement, the front foot would be at 12 o'clock). These men have a good point. Their exaggerated windup forces them to have excellent shoulder rotation which, so the theory goes, helps add RPM's to the racquet head—plus their almost flailing motion disguises the ultimate direction of the delivery.

I have been unsuccessful in various experiments with my serve. For example, I have been criticized for my toss, which is too high and nearly straight above my body instead of one lower, out to the side, and inside the court. I am told the bio-mechanic graphs show that maximum power can only be achieved by throwing the ball out to the side so that the swing comes across the body, not up and down.

My ball toss is so high it is out of the frame, yet my weight distribution forward is gradual and not reckless. My rotating and dropping my right shoulder assure good power.

The game's biggest servers, John McEnroe, Roscoe Tanner, and John Newcombe, have optimum power and spin from lower tosses, to the side and in front of their lead foot. My serve and toss, on the other hand, defies the accepted wis-

dom—particularly the high toss which is hell to control in the wind—yet it has gotten better and better and is now one of the most feared on the tour. This is another one of those times when you

Good extension of my right arm. Toe pirouette assures I am hitting the ball at the top of the toss.

must be ready to buck the experts and do what works for you.

One of the standard myths is that you don't have to have a good serve to win on clay (which is

true); but its corollary, that a good serve can't be a weapon on clay, is totally false. I serve more aces on any surface, but particularly on clay, than any of the world's top ten players. I think the rewards of taking the risk and going for the line on a first serve are obvious. You may fire an ace or put your foe in so much trouble that he can't get back into the point.

You don't get many chances to finish the point on clay without running. Shooting for an ace or near ace is one way. Moreover, there is less risk in

The classic "scissors kick" movement, right foot over left.

going for a "big one" on a slow surface than on a
fast surface where the percentages of three-quar-
ter-paced first serves are tactically important to
keep the counterpuncher away from the net. But
on clay no one dares return a second serve and
charge the net on a regular basis, so there is no
penalty for missing the first serve.

One of the most misunderstood theories in tennis is the benefit of getting a high percentage of
first serves in. In doubles, the theory is inevitably
correct: There is less court for the server to cover

The service follow-through. Note high elbow—the result of upward arm thrust and final wrist snap at ball.

on his way to the net, so he just needs a delivery that the returner can't take advantage of. In other words, you don't want to give your opponents much of a look at your second serve. In singles the first serve count is often meaningless. Statistics are now kept of first serve percentages in every Grand Prix and WCT match, and approximately 50 percent of the winners for the random six tournaments I reviewed had worse serving percentages than the losers. For instance, in the Houston WCT, against Clerc in the final, my percentage was 40—his was far better—but I won nearly all of those 40 percent points. A week later, in the Dallas finals against Vijay Amritraj, I served at almost a 95 percent accuracy in the first set and 100 percent in the second set. But I didn't hit an ace. Or even close. I was just pushing my first serve in because I didn't want to hurt my arm for the next day against McEnroe. Yet everybody said "wow" at the perfect percentage. It was totally irrelevant.

SERVICE RETURN

To me, the more important statistic is percentage of service returns made. A high number of safe service returns is a far more accurate barometer of good performance than first serves. The good service returners—Borg, Connors, Vilas, McEnroe, and myself—don't go for the outright winner unless forced to by a serve that's drawn us far out of court where a mediocre return will surely lose the point. Gambling at this stage is like using the doubling cube in backgammon. If you

The conclusion of the service follow-through. The scissors kick of right foot over left is complete, the racquet moves across the body, and the left foot kicks up in the air much in the same way as a baseball pitcher's rear foot shoots up as a natural reaction and balancing action to the powerful forward thrust of the entire body.

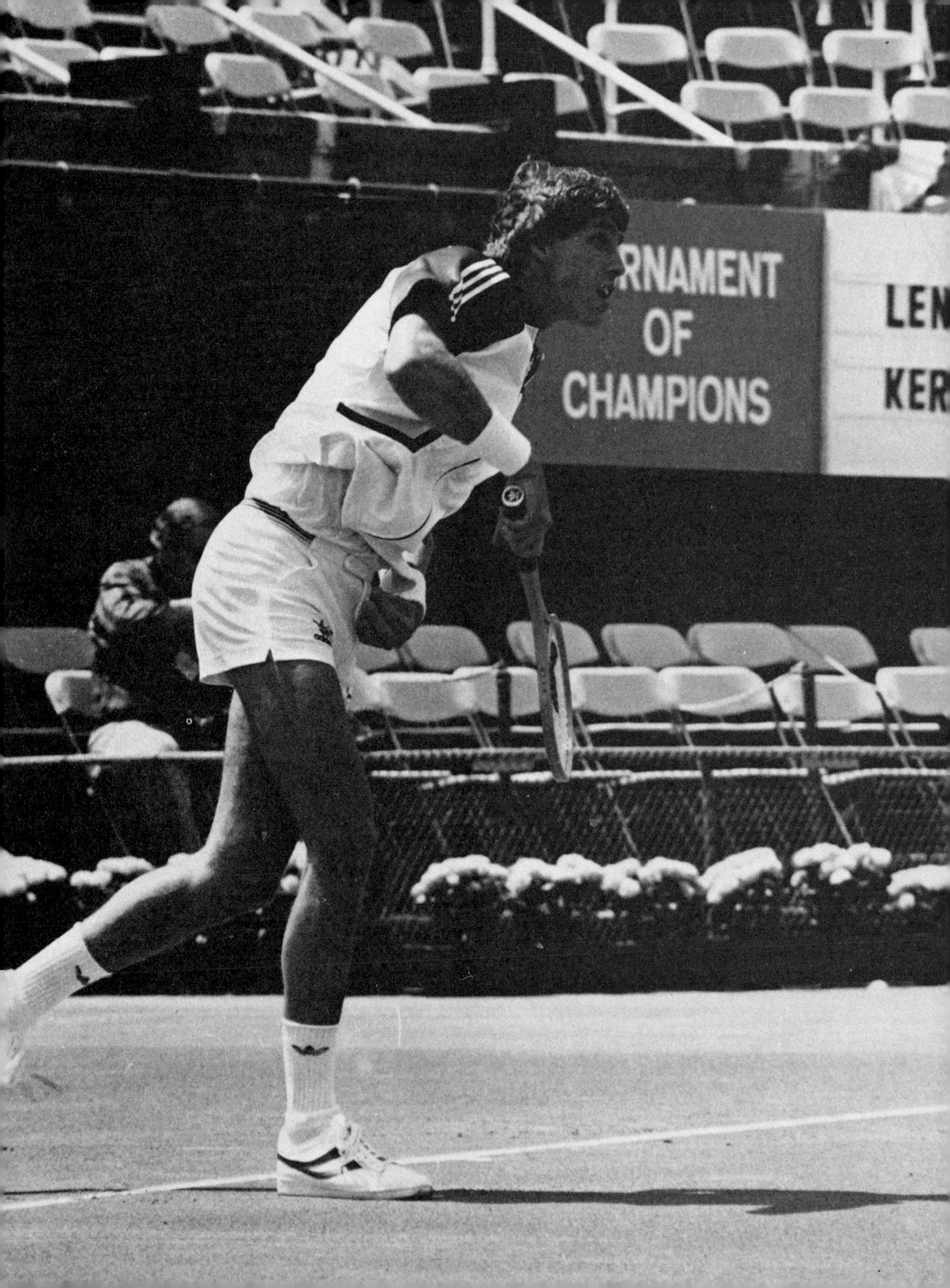
RNAMENT
OF
CHAMPIONS
LEN
KER

Occasionally, on a second serve, the right foot will not "scissor" over the left.

have only a 20 percent chance of hitting an out-right winner, those are better odds than a 100 percent safe return where you have no possibility of winning the point.

The success of any super-pro's return lies in two not-so-simple elements, power and consistency. Power blunts the volleyer's offense and pins the groundstroker to the baseline. Consistency—most often in the form of exceptional topspin (except for Connors, who relies on uncanny timing and precision)—complements the purpose of power. The ball dips at the netman's feet, forcing him to volley up or the ball to bounce high to the baseline, neutralizing his groundstrokes.

Patience is at a premium on the return. Nothing is as uplifting psychologically to a server as seeing his opponent return into the bottom of the net. Make sure you put your return in play (unless you're playing John McEnroe at your club and his serve pulls you out into the alley). Seriously, most players assume that because they're facing a big serve-volleyer they must do something extra special with the return. Don't be silly. If the guy gets his strong serve in, just getting the return back should be enough. If he could hit both serve and volley for winners without missing, he'd be on the tour. Remember, consistency is the core to the service return.

A server's greatest frustration is seeing his best effort returned harmlessly in a semi arc that lands a foot inside the baseline. He feels cheated that he hasn't won the point outright and usually responds by looking for instant gratification—a poor percentage pounding for the sideline. Feed the server's sense of futility by getting every return in play.

And even after the point is under way and the server has made his way to net, you should understand that the volley is the most difficult shot in tennis to master. The volley is supposed to be the killing shot—the "concluder." But few players can do more than rally with their volley. By understanding this limitation, you can improve your own percentages by avoiding the off-balance or out-of-position passing shot. Wait for your best chance of hitting the pass. In the meantime, you can help set up this opportunity by returning low and not giving your opponent anything above the net to swat.

Unlike the typical aggressive player, I never stand on top of the baseline to return serve. On a fast surface—grass, concrete, or any of the asphalt-based surfaces like Deco Turf II used at the U.S. Open—I stand at least three feet behind the baseline leaning forward. On clay I move even farther back because it is not so important to return the ball quickly.

And unlike the recommendation of the old-time superstars like Jack Kramer and Don Budge, who advise holding the racquet with the forehand grip while waiting for the serve, I wait with the backhand grip with the racquet leaning in that direction. The reasons are simple. The backhand takes more time to prepare and execute than the forehand, plus most players serve more often to the backhand.

One important tip. In the juniors I had trouble returning everyone's serve. I discovered I was watching my opponent rather than his ball toss. This problem can be more troublesome in a baseline rally, the effect of which can be hypnotizing and can lull you into tracking your rival's

movements rather than the ball. Another thing:
On the return, lean forward as the server starts his
windup. This will get your juices flowing early and
will put your weight on the balls of your feet so
that you can step into the ball quickly. It also saves
time so that you're not forced to set the racquet
back into position at the last second. You will also
notice that I don't bounce up and down madly
while waiting to return. There is instead a small
hop as the server tosses the ball up, which puts
me on "ready alert."

Anyone 'Round My Net Is It

*U*nderstanding the technique of my volley is not as important as knowing what role the volley plays in my overall game. I am not a server and volleyer. And despite well-wishers, I don't think I ever will be one. I do, however, partially base my offensive on a serve that wins points outright or that draws a weak return that begs to be put away by the forehand—or that causes a floater that my volley can pounce on.

I hit the backhand volley with racquet head high, elbow fairly straight. Contact is made well in front of my right shoulder. Left hand is in perfect balancing position, indicating there was ample time to place the volley carefully.

I will never be a player like McEnroe whose volley creates openings followed by the sudden kill. My serve or groundstrokes create the opening, and my volley merely terminates the point. But make no mistake, my volley is not really responsible for winning the point.

My grip is orthodox: the backhand for both sides unless I have a lot of time to switch grips to the forehand for a swinging volley. I don't take a full backswing, but I do hit the ball with full force if the ball is chest high—which should be a helpful suggestion to those of you who have difficulty putting any volley away. I do keep the racquet face high, I bend well for low balls, and I have good reach, which makes it difficult to pass me. My shortcomings are critical. I'm a steady rather than an aggressive volleyer. I don't miss, but I don't put the ball away unless my groundstrokes or serve have set me up.

Furthermore, my hands at the net are not as quick as McEnroe's, Gerulaitis' or Gottfried's, so I prefer to stay where my strengths are—in the

When time allows—which isn't often—the forehand volley is also hit well in front of the body and off the left front foot. Photo on page 98, right, shows importance of maintaining body control at the net in anticipation of the next shot. Note that right elbow is bent, racquet face high.

backcourt until my rival is totally (and helplessly) on the defensive. There is another vital time when I come to net—as a change of pace or for a surprise attack. Don't confuse the two. There is an overlap, but each has its own tactical nuance. A surprise attack—a quick return and rush to net— would be effective at break point; a change of pace—serve and volley—at 15-all. Certainly my volley will improve; but the foundation of my game has been built in the backcourt, and not in the usual sense of the baseline idiom which is defensive and running. My backcourt methodology is total offense, but there is also a sense of patience, of waiting for the short ball to attack.

Why won't I change to a serve-volleyer? I think there are inherent risks in tinkering with a structure that has taken me almost twenty years to assemble. Ion Tiriac, Guillermo Vilas' alter ego (and manager), has tried to convert his charge to a volleyer, with mixed results. Understand your strengths. Work on your weaknesses just so that they can't be exploited, but not with a mind to

I am more comfortable with the high forehand volley than any others, because technique is not at a premium. I can swing away almost in the same manner as a high forehand at the baseline.

These are the only photos not taken in the heat of an actual match. You can see the lack of intensity from my facial expression. (You may even detect a trace of a smile?) The casualness does not mean that the technique is incorrect. In all photos the racquet head is tilted with an open face to impart underspin (for control). Three of these photos show that when balls come straight at the body, the backhand is used—never the forehand—because it is much easier to swing or to block the backhand in front of the body. In these warm-up pictures the emphasis is on trying to get a feel for the ball rather than on aggressively putting each shot away.

making them your strengths—else you chance losing the weapon that created you.

THE OVERHEAD

The adage that the overhead is just like the serve I find to be almost totally false. There are few similarities. For instance, how can the serve be like the overhead when most overheads are hit at least twenty feet in front of where every serve is struck? The angles and purposes of each stroke are far apart. Some superstars like Vitas Gerulaitis have better overheads than serves. The reason is clear. Vitas has worked extremely hard perfecting

his serve but it still gives him trouble. Yet when he is not restricted to hitting his serve into one small box seventy-eight feet away, his motion is loose and forceful.

One of the keys to a good overhead is the trailing foot. It plays a more dominant role than the front foot, though Vitas and I are often not proper examples of foot positioning on the overhead. The right foot (for right-handers) should be way behind the left foot in a stance that is similar to the quarterback's throwing position at the time his arm is cocked. All weight is placed on that right leg which is bent to give maximum push when the forward motion starts.

Since the net is not the same obstacle to the overhead as it is for the serve, the overhead should unleash an almost reckless power. Control and accuracy to within a few inches are not as important as with the serve. And the weaker the lob, the less important overhead accuracy becomes; for the angles open up to allow a "bounce" putaway in any direction.

There is one more difference between serve and overhead. On the serve you can toss the ball to your favorite spot. If it's not perfect you can catch the toss and try again. Not so with the overhead where your opponent is arranging the toss and it's not in his interest to make it so perfect. So, in effect, you'll see topspin and underspin tosses, high and low tosses. In an instant you have to decide whether to let the ball bounce or hit it in the air, whether to hit an overhead or a high forehand—or the most difficult shot of all, the backhand overhead.

Furthermore, the racquet should be taken back

Because the overhead is hit close to the net where power and taking the lob quickly are so important, preparation is seldom as careful as for service. I don't always have time to line up my left foot firmly in front of my right—left shoulder pointing at the net. Nor is it always possible (or preferable) to scissors kick right foot over left on the overhead. In these photos, I was caught by surprise and am directly facing the net. But I am tall enough to make the adjustment quickly, get full extension on my racquet arm, and follow through across my body.

and held in a cocked position the minute the ball is in the air—unlike the serve which unwinds in one continuous motion. And since it is easier to run forward than backward to make last minute adjustments to sun or wind, it is best to move back a step or two more than where you antici- pate hitting the ball. One last thing. You get two chances to hit a serve, so you see I don't think it has much in common with the overhead at all.

The Force

*D*eveloping my power game was not a deliberate act. It happened almost by accident. Perhaps even a genetic accident—for when I was a teenager I was not that tall or strong and I didn't hit the ball particularly hard. I had an underspin backhand which was very vulnerable. I concealed the weakness by coming to net on everything so I'd never have to pass from my backhand—which I simply couldn't do.

But I did work hard during those years and I got stronger and stronger. I made a particular effort on the backhand—staying low to the ball and learning to come over its face rather than cut down defensively. One of the things that now makes my shots look even faster is the contrast with my off-pace ball. In other words, I don't hit out on every stroke unless I get a good bounce and good speed. I'll wait for the right shot before I really go for it. The other side of patience is comfort. If I'm off balance or I get a bad bounce, I'll wait. It is important to be comfortable and not rushed if you're trying for maximum speed and accuracy. Believe me, be patient; you'll get ample opportunity to hit the perfect pass, but until then be content to do what tennis originally intended us all to do—just rally.

Occasionally if I'm out of position, I may be aggressive because my other choices are zero, but normally I bide my time waiting for the short ball to attack, which explains why to date I haven't

The follow-through on service, short forehand, and backhand show the strain and force of each shot (facing and following pages).

been too successful against Jimmy Connors. He never hits short. He keeps me pinned to the baseline where I can't overpower him. Yet I have a strong record against Borg and McEnroe, who do give me short balls to counterpunch. The lesson is an important one. Don't assume that because you beat Sam, and Sam thrashes Harry, you'll mop up Harry. Match-ups are very important in tennis. Your strength may be a forehand down-the-line approach that plays right into the hands of an opponent with a fabulous backhand passing shot. What is called for, naturally, is an adjustment in your game which may demand that you revert to a pattern you are not at home with.

It sounds incredible but of all the skills that tennis requires, one of the most important, but most ignored, is resourcefulness. And I'm as guilty as my fellow pros. For example, often when I get in a tight situation against Connors or McEnroe, I won't change my game; I will just try to do what I have been doing better. I will try to concentrate more or hit the ball with more force, but seldom will I alter my style to disorient my opponent. I have been lucky so far to get away with such stubbornness—but that may not always be the case. The first time I was really stung by this habit was at the 1982 French Open. I was expected to win it but was upset by the young Swedish sensation, Mats Wilander. Instead of being patient and waiting for the openings, I tried to end the point quickly. After all, this strategy had worked two weeks earlier against Eddie Dibbs in the WCT Forest Hills final. I beat Eddie 6-0, 6-1 in under 50 minutes, but the clay at the West Side Tennis Club is faster than in Paris. Wilander had more time to run down each ball. I didn't make the adjustment and paid dearly for my hard-headedness.

Basically, on those days when I am impatient, I am not as good a player on clay as on hard courts where a big, risky groundstroke is rewarded by the point outright instead of a neutralizing retrieve.

We all hear plenty of conversation about who is better—the current pros or the heroes of yesteryear. I think the comparison is impossible. The fairest test is accomplishment. How many Wimbledons did Bill Tilden win compared to Jimmy Connors or Bjorn Borg? This gives the superior records of men and women a perpetual place in the game's history.

If I were to be less fair and less diplomatic, however, and measure skill on the current measurable standards—speed, power, agility—I don't think the older guys would stand a chance. It has been said by many, including Jack Kramer, that Don Budge was the greatest player who ever lived. His Grand Slam feat was unique and his place in our sport's archives is confirmed, but he simply shouldn't be judged by modern measures. Nevertheless, many of the former greats insist on that comparison, and when they do I jump in with both feet.

I know the famous Australian Davis cup captain Harry Hopman has said that if Bill Tilden played John McEnroe today on the Centre Court of Wimbledon that Tilden would win. I don't. I think Tilden would be looking for games—he'd need a microscope.

I have firm views about the oversize racquet too. I think the Prince size is great for beginners and seniors; and it may help some pros, but it will not bring them to the very top. Gene Mayer has made excellent use of the oversize racquet, and it has maximized his talent because his swing is short. My racquet is slightly larger than conventional and is made of graphite and fiberglass. I need a "fast" racquet so that I can move the head quickly and with speed for maximum topspin and velocity. The larger the racquet head the more stable it is at the center, which means you can't maneuver it rapidly.

Many of my friends have asked me why I don't play doubles. Does it mean I have no aptitude for the game? I think I have talent for doubles. In 1980, after all, I was ranked in the world's top 10 in doubles with Fibak. However, the doubles schedule interferes with singles. Doubles are always the last matches of the day, when it's cold and almost dark. You're tired and prone to injury. At indoor tournaments, it's worse, with matches often being scheduled after 1 A.M. because of the limited court space. Besides, the whole structure of tennis is to reward and honor the single best player—the singles player. We all recall that Bjorn Borg won the French Open a record six times. Do you know who won the doubles championship in any of those years?

My personal training regimen is austere, though not as tough as Borg's. In preparing for a tournament, I do run for 30 minutes before breakfast each day—jogging for endurance to take me through a four-hour match and sprinting for necessary speed for the short, quick steps required on court. I do no weight training, although I know many have great success with various lightweight exercises in building both stamina and strength. But I train hard on court, three to four hours each day.

I do adjust my schedule to what I think my game requires in terms of drilling or playing sets. And I warm up thoroughly on the day of my matches—usually twice in half-hour sessions. I am somewhat spoiled in that I don't have to watch what I eat. It's lucky that what I want to eat is good for me. I perform the usual pasta ritual twenty-four hours before a match, and my breakfast beforehand is enormous—three or four eggs, ham, toast, and fruit. And then an hour or so before, I have a sandwich. Perhaps a pivotal part of competition is getting away as soon as the last game is over each day. I go home and read and listen to music to unwind and forget the tension.

The sawdust fetish you witness when I'm on court is just a matter of storing a fistful of sawdust in my right pocket to dry my racquet hand. After every point on a sunny day I fill my right hand with the sawdust which absorbs the sweat and falls to the ground. On grass or clay, this routine is not noticed, but on the U.S. Open hardcourts, the material collects behind the baseline and officials have now assigned a sweeper to clean up after me.

My expression on court is somewhat dour and serious. But that's my way of blocking out the million distractions in the stands, the press box, and the court next to me. The silent, solemn look I present is part of the concentration process.

*"Ivan will not show his real face on the court be-
cause tennis is his profession. He wants to be Ivan
Lendl, superstar. Number 1. He wants to be cool
because that's his protection. If he would sudden-
ly open himself up, he might be hurt somewhere.
By being hard and cruel he's not asking the public
to like him, just respect him."*
Wojtek Fibak to New York Times *sportswriter Neil
Amdur*